NATURAL WONDERS

The Great Lakes

The Largest Group of Lakes in the World

Annalise Bekkering

WEIGL PUBLISHERS INC.

Published by Weigl Publishers Inc.
350 5th Avenue, Suite 3304, PMB 6G
New York, NY 10118-0069

Website: www.weigl.com

Library of Congress Cataloging-in-Publication Data

Bekkering, Annalise.
 The Great Lakes / Annalise Bekkering.
         p. cm. – (Natural wonders)
Includes index.
ISBN 978-59036-944-9 (hard cover: alk. Paper)—ISBN 978-1-59036-945-6 (soft cover: alk. Paper) 1. Great Lakes (North America)—Juvenile literature. 2. Great Lakes Region (North America)—Juvenile literature. 3. Great Lakes Region (North America)—Geography—Juvenile literature. I. Title.
F551.b45 2008
977—dc22

2008015664

Printed in the United States of America
1 2 3 4 5 6 7 8 9 0   12 11 10 09 08

Project Coordinators
Heather Kissock and
Heather C. Hudak

Design
Terry Paulhus

Photograph Credits

Weigl acknowledges Getty Images as its primary image supplier.

MODIS Rapid Response Team, NASA Goddard Space Flight Center Images captured by the MODIS instrument on board the Terra or Aqua satellite: page 4; NOAA, Great Lakes Environmental Research Laboratory: page 19; U.S. Fish and Wildlife Service: pages 12, 13.

Every reasonable effort has been made to trace ownership and to obtain permission to reprint copyright material. The publishers would be pleased to have any errors or omissions brought to their attention so that they may be corrected in subsequent printings.

Contents

The Magnificent Lakes

The Great Lakes include Lakes Huron, Ontario, Michigan, Erie, and Superior. They form the largest group of lakes in the world. The Great Lakes contain a large portion of Earth's fresh water and are home to many plants and animals. These living things depend on the unique **ecosystems** that make up the Great Lakes and their surrounding area for their survival.

The Great Lakes have a rich history. Aboriginal Peoples have lived in the area for thousands of years. Europeans settled in the area in the 1600s. The five lakes are within the United States and Canada. Both countries work together to protect this natural wonder of the world.

The Great Lakes hold about 21 percent of the world's fresh water.

Great Lakes Facts

- The Great Lakes contain 6 **quadrillion** gallons (23 quadrillion liters) of fresh water. This is enough to cover the entire United States with water 9.5 feet (2.9 meters) deep.

- The shoreline of the Great Lakes is about 10,000 miles (16,000 kilometers) long. This is 44 percent of Earth's **circumference**.

- About 30 percent of Canada's population and 10 percent of the United States' population live in the **Great Lakes Basin**.

- Lake Superior is the largest of the Great Lakes. It is so large that it could hold all the water from the other four lakes, plus three more lakes the size of Lake Erie.

- Lake Superior is the deepest of the Great Lakes. The deepest point in Lake Superior is 1,332 feet (406 m).

- Lake Erie contains the least amount of water of the five Great Lakes. Lake Ontario is the smallest in area.

Great Lakes Locator

Where in the World?

The Great Lakes are located in central North America. They are surrounded by the Canadian province of Ontario, and the U.S. states of Illinois, Indiana, Michigan, Minnesota, New York, Ohio, Pennsylvania, and Wisconsin. Lake Michigan is the only lake entirely within the United States. The other four lakes straddle the border between Canada and the United States. Four large cities—Chicago, Detroit, Toronto, and Cleveland—are found on the banks of the Great Lakes. The Great Lakes are important to the **economy** and trade of these cities.

All of the Great Lakes are connected by a series of rivers, straits, and canals. St. Mary's River connects Lakes Superior and Huron, while the Straits of Mackinac connect Lakes Huron and Michigan. Lake Huron flows into Lake Erie though Lake Saint Clair and the Detroit River. Lake Erie uses the Niagara River to connect to Lake Ontario.

■ **Chicago is located on the shore of Lake Michigan.**

Puzzler

Q One Canadian province and eight American states surround the Great Lakes. Where are these states and province located? See if you can match the letters to the numbers on the map.

A. New York   D. Indiana   G. Minnesota
B. Ontario   E. Ohio   H. Illinois
C. Pennsylvania   F. Michigan   I. Wisconsin

A 1) B 2) G 3) I 4) H 5) D 6) F 7) E 8) C 9) A

A Trip Back in Time

The Great Lakes began to form during the **Pleistocene Epoch**. Huge sheets of ice called glaciers moved from the north to what is now the Great Lakes region. The glaciers **eroded** the land as they moved, flattening mountains and hills and creating large valleys.

As the glaciers melted and moved, large dents were left in the land. Over thousands of years, the climate became warmer, and the glaciers slowly began to melt away. The dents in the land were filled with melted water from the glaciers. These water-filled holes became the Great Lakes.

■ **A glacier is made of ice, snow, water, rock, and dirt. Some of the glaciers that covered the Great Lakes region were 6,500 feet (2,000 m) thick in places.**

How Glaciers Shape the Land

Gravity causes glaciers to move. It makes them twist and slide down slopes. Glaciers move very slowly, in some cases only 1 to 2 feet (30 to 60 centimeters) per day. They erode and shape the land as they travel.

When a glacier travels over land, it picks up rocks and **sediment** in some places and deposits them in others. Mounds of sediment deposited by a glacier are called moraines. Drumlins are hills of sediment that are made when a glacier retreats. Eskers are thin ridges of sediment formed by water running underneath a glacier.

■ Drumlins formed by glaciers can be found in Wisconsin.

■ Eskers are often many miles long.

Plant Life in the Great Lakes

At one time, tallgrass prairies, forests, grasslands, and bogs surrounded the Great Lakes. However, the landscape around the Great Lakes changed when settlers arrived about 400 years ago.

In some places, plants have been cleared for farmland or to build communities. Logging was a major industry in the area in the 1800s. Trees were cut down to make furniture, ships, and homes. No new trees were planted to replace those that had been taken. Many forests have been lost.

Today, common plants in the Great Lakes region include wildflowers, pine trees, and oak trees. These plants thrive in the Great Lakes climate. People have brought a number of new plants to the Great Lakes region. These plants can harm native plants that naturally belong in the region by taking over their habitat.

▬ **Industries are now a major feature along the Great Lakes.**

The Michigan Monkey Flower

The Michigan monkey flower grows in cold, flowing spring water along shorelines in Michigan's Great Lakes region. The bright-yellow, tube-shaped flower grows between 0.6 and 1.06 inches (16 and 27 millimeters) high.

The Michigan monkey flower is an **endangered species**. Human activity, such as building near streams, is a major threat to the flower. Such activity destroys the plant's habitat and the springs that the flower needs to survive. In order to save this plant, sources of spring water need to be protected.

■ Monkey flowers are said to look like a monkey's face.

Great Lakes Animals

The Great Lakes are rich in animal life. Some of these animals are native to the area. Others have been brought to the region by humans. These animals compete with each other for food and habitat. Moose, black bears, lynx, and wolves live in the northern parts of the area, near Lakes Superior, Michigan, and Huron. Owls, squirrels, and white-tailed deer can be found living in the forests around the lower Great Lakes region.

Many types of fish, such as lake trout, walleye, brook trout, yellow perch, and muskellunge, live within the waters of the Great Lakes. These fish feed on the insects, plankton, and plants that live in and around the water.

The Great Lakes provide birds with food and nesting areas. Birds found around the Great Lakes include the American bittern, great blue heron, double-crested cormorant, wood thrush, and the grasshopper sparrow. The lakes are also used as resting stops by **migratory** birds, such as Canada geese.

■ **The Karner blue butterfly is one of the many rare animals living within the Great Lakes ecosystem.**

Giant of the Great Lakes

Lake sturgeon have lived in the Great Lakes since the **Ice Age**. As the largest fish in the Great Lakes, they can weigh up to 300 pounds (136 kilograms) and be 8 feet (2.5 m) long. Lake sturgeon are bottom-feeders. They use their vacuum-like mouth to suck up insects and **crustaceans** from the bottom of the lake.

Human contact has greatly affected lake sturgeon. Early American Indians used these fish for food, oil, and leather. In the 1800s, fishers began to catch lake sturgeon for commercial use. By the 1900s, the lake sturgeon population was very low due to over-fishing. To bring back the population, the Canadian and U.S. governments named the fish a threatened animal. Now, there are many restrictions on fishing for lake sturgeon.

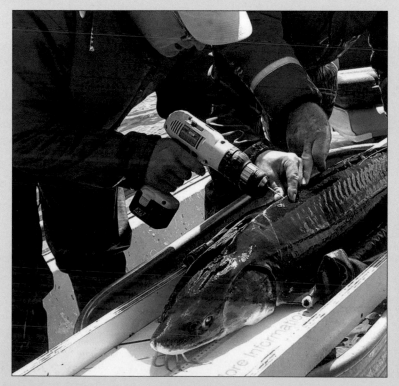

■ **Fish and wildlife officers tag lake sturgeon so they can keep track of their numbers.**

Early Settlement

Aboriginal Peoples have lived in the Great Lakes region for centuries. With its large supply of fresh water, fertile land, and diverse plant and animal species, the area is rich in resources. Early Aboriginal Peoples were able to live in the area by hunting, fishing, and growing squash, corn, and other vegetables.

In the 1500s and 1600s, Europeans began to explore the Great Lakes area. The first Europeans to arrive were French explorers and fur traders. They were soon followed by explorers and fur traders from Great Britain. Both groups built the fur trade in the region. They used the lakes to transport furs to trading posts.

Over time, European settlers began to move into the area. They set up farms, towns, and villages around the lakes. Some of these settlements grew to become major American and Canadian cities.

▬ **Milwaukee, Wisconsin, began as a fur trade post. The city is located along Lake Michigan.**

Biography

Samuel de Champlain (1567–1635)

Samuel de Champlain was a French explorer. He first traveled to North America in 1603 on a fur-trading mission. Champlain soon became one of the most important explorers of the Great Lakes.

In 1615, Champlain and his group explored Lake Ontario and Georgian Bay, part of Lake Huron. He spent the winter with a group of local Aboriginal Peoples called the Huron. While there, Champlain asked the Huron about the land to the west. They told him that there were vast lakes beyond Lake Huron. However, they advised Champlain against traveling there because of an ongoing war between Aboriginal groups in the West. Champlain agreed and, instead, he used information provided by the Huron to make a map of the Great Lakes. Although his map was unfinished, it was the first geographical information about the eastern Great Lakes.

Facts of Life

Born: 1567

Hometown: Brouage, France

Occupation: Explorer

Died: December 25, 1635

The Big Picture

Freshwater lakes are home to many kinds of animals and provide drinking water to large numbers of people. This map shows where some of the world's largest freshwater lakes are found.

PACIFIC
OCEAN

NORTH
AMERICA

ATLANTIC
OCEAN

SOUTH
AMERICA

1 **Lake Baikal in Russia** is the deepest lake in the world. It holds one-fifth of the world's fresh surface water.

2 **Lake Tanganyika in Africa** is the longest freshwater lake in the world. It is 420 miles (680 km) long.

3 **Lake Victoria in Africa** is the second-largest freshwater lake in the world. It drains into the Mediterranean Sea through the Nile River.

4 **Lake Malawi in Africa** is 1,550 feet (472 m) above sea level. It lies between the African countries of Malawi, Tanzania, and Mozambique.

5 **The Great Lakes** are the largest system of fresh surface water in the world. The lakes span more than 750 miles (1,200 km) from west to east.

6 **Great Slave Lake in Canada** is the deepest lake in North America. Its deepest point is 2,015 feet (614 m).

The Great Lakes Today

When European settlers came to live in the area around the Great Lakes, they learned of the resources the region had to offer. Settlers used these resources to develop industries, such as agriculture, logging, and fishing. Word of the riches found there quickly made its way back to Europe and other places. People began **immigrating** to the Great Lakes region. This helped the area to develop further.

Today, about 40 million people live in the Great Lakes region. Most of these people live along the mouths of rivers and canals connected to the Great Lakes. Communities grew in these places because of the easy access to shipping and fresh water.

Resources found in the Great Lakes region are still used for businesses. Many people in the Great Lakes Basin work in agriculture, manufacturing, mining, and shipping. Major industries in the Great Lakes region include steel, paper, chemical, and automobile production. About 80,000 people work in the sport and commercial fishing industry.

▬ Detroit is also known as the "Motor City" for its strong automobile industry.

The Environment

The Great Lakes region is one of the most largely populated areas in North America. When such a large number of people live in one place, there can be a huge effect on the environment.

The Environmental Research Laboratory was created in 1974 in Ann Arbor, Michigan, to study life in and around the Great Lakes. Its goal is to research the environment and ecosystems of the Great Lakes and provide ideas for restoring and protecting them.

A main focus of the laboratory is the study of pollution within the Great Lakes. Scientists observe the types and levels of pollution that enter the area. They study the effects that this pollution has on the people, plants, and animals that call the region home.

Scientists at the laboratory study the effect **invasive species** have on native species and the Great Lakes ecosystem. Research is being done to assess the impact that climate change might have on the Great Lakes.

Field scientists assess the Great Lakes' waters.

Natural Attractions

Each year, more than 250 million tourists visit the Great Lakes. Some come to take part in the outdoor activities. Others come to see the sights. The Great Lakes have plenty of activities for each season of the year. In the winter, people can go ice fishing, skiing, and snowmobiling. In the summer, golfing, swimming, fishing, and boating are common activities for tourists and the people who live in the area. Many summer tourists enjoy swimming in the waters of Great Lakes and relaxing on the sandy beaches.

Tourists flock to the area in autumn to see trees change from their summer green to the deep red and orange of the season. National, state, and provincial parks are located all around the lakes.

Off Whitefish Point in Lake Superior, tourists can go diving among shipwrecks. At this site, known as the "graveyard of the Great Lakes," more than 300 ships have been lost to storms. Divers can view these shipwrecks and catch a glimpse of the plants and animals that live in the waters.

▬ **The Apostle Islands are sometimes called the "Jewels of Lake Superior."**

The *Edmund Fitzgerald*

On November 9, 1975, the S.S. *Edmund Fitzgerald* left port in Superior, Wisconsin, headed for Detroit. The ship was traveling across Lake Superior with a full load of cargo. November is known as "the month of storms" in the Great Lakes. A fierce storm hit on November 10, sending 30-foot (9.1-m) high waves over the deck of the ship. The waves damaged the ship's water pumps and destroyed life rafts. That night, the *Edmund Fitzgerald* sank, taking the lives of the 29 crewmembers aboard.

The sinking of the *Edmund Fitzgerald* is one of the great mysteries of the Great Lakes. There are many theories about what caused the shipwreck, but none has been proven. The boat lies 530 feet

(161 m) deep in Lake Superior, broken in half. The *Edmund Fitzgerald* is one of the best-known shipwrecks in history.

Divers recovered the ship's bell in 1995. It was restored and is displayed in the Great Lakes Shipwreck Museum in Michigan. Every year on November 10, the bell is rung in memory of the crew and the ship.

■ **Today, a lighthouse stands at Whitefish Point, Michigan, where the *Edmund Fitzgerald* sank.**

Great Lakes Legends

Aboriginal Peoples have a special relationship with the Great Lakes. They have created many legends about how the lakes were formed. These stories have been passed down through generations.

One Huron legend tells the story about Kitchikewana, a giant god who protected Lake Huron's Georgian Bay. Kitchikewana had a terrible temper because he was very lonely. He wanted a beautiful girl named Wanakita to be his bride, but she was not interested in him. Wanakita was in love with a warrior from her tribe.

Kitchikewana became very angry. He dug his fingers into the ground and picked up large handfuls of dirt. He threw the dirt into the Georgian Bay. The dirt became small islands within the bay. The fingermarks he left in the sand became five smaller bays.

After his tantrum, Kitchikewana was tired. He crashed to the ground, fell asleep, and never rose again. Today, it is said that Kitchikewana's body can be seen sleeping on Giant's Tomb, Georgian Bay's largest island.

▬ In his rage, Kitchikewana accidentally killed the daughter of an Aboriginal chief. It is said that silver birch grow on Beausoliel Island to honor her memory.

Recipe

Bannock is a type of bread. British settlers brought their recipe for bannock to North America and introduced it to Aboriginal Peoples throughout the continent. It became a staple for many Aboriginal Peoples. With the help of an adult, you can make bannock to share with your friends and family.

You will need:

2 cups flour
2 tbsp baking powder
2 tbsp sugar
a pinch of salt
6 ounces water

What to do:

1. Preheat oven to 425° Fahrenheit (220° Celsius).

2. In a bowl, whisk together flour, baking powder, sugar, and salt. Add water, and knead into dough. If too dry, add more water, 1 tablespoon at a time.

3. With your hands, mold the dough into eight 3-inch (76-mm) circles, each about 0.2 inch (5 mm) thick. Place the circles on a greased baking sheet.

4. Bake until lightly browned, about 20 minutes.

5. Remove from oven, let cool, and enjoy.

Protecting the Lakes

Human activities, such as farming and fishing, have impacted the Great Lakes ecosystem. The Canadian and U.S. governments have worked together to protect the Great Lakes. Still, pollution and invasive species pose a big threat to the plants and animals that live there.

Water stays in the Great Lakes for a long time. This means pollutants, such as pesticides and fertilizers, that get into the lake stay for a long time as well. They have time to cause damage to the plants and animals living there. Pollutants also have made large **algae** blooms, especially in Lake Erie. The algae uses up much of the oxygen in the water. Many fish and water animals do not get the oxygen they need to survive.

▬ **Industrial waste contains chemicals that harm water quality. Fish living in this polluted water are unsafe to eat.**

Animals and plants within the Great Lakes region are threatened by invasive species. These plants and animals take food and habitat away from native species. Since 1830, more than 140 invasive species have entered the Great Lakes. Many have been brought into the area in the water that moves along with ships. These species have had a big impact on the 130 endangered and rare plants and animals found within the Great Lakes.

Should the governments limit pesticide and fertilizer use around the Great Lakes?

YES	NO
Pollution can kill fish and plants in the lakes.	Many people rely on these industries for jobs and income. 
 Pollution in the water is eaten by fish. These fish may harm humans who eat them.	Even though agriculture uses pesticides and fertilizers, it does so to provide people with food.
Controlling pollution can help increase the populations of threatened species.	Scientists can find chemicals that are less polluting to the Great Lakes.

Timeline

10,000 years ago
The Ice Age ends, and the Great Lakes begin to form.

1615
Samuel de Champlain explores Lakes Ontario and Huron.

1622
French explorer Étienne Brûlé explores Lake Superior.

1634
French explorer Jean Nicolet is the first European to see Lake Michigan.

1669
French explorer Louis Joliet discovers Lake Erie.

1850–1880
Large forests in the Great Lakes region are lost due to logging.

1860s
The first paper mill is developed in the Great Lakes region. Waste from the mill is dumped in the lakes as pollution.

Yachts are a common sight on Lake Michigan.

1909
Canada and the United States form a joint commission to share responsibility for the Great Lakes.

1959
The St. Lawrence Seaway opens, connecting the Great Lakes to the Atlantic Ocean and increasing shipping through the Great Lakes.

Some people enjoy camping on the shore of Lake Huron.

Big Tub Harbour is the site of more than 20 sunken ships.

Canada lynx live across Canada and the northern United States.

1975
The Edmund Fitzgerald sinks in Lake Superior.

1980s–1990s
Chemical pollution is reduced, but the number of invasive species continues to increase.

1987
The Canadian and United States governments create plans to clean up threatened areas.

2002
The Great Lakes Legacy Act is developed. It provides $270 million dollars over five years to clean the lakes and educate people about protecting them.

1970s
Toxic chemicals, such as DDT and PCBs, become a concern for environmental and human health. The dumping of these chemicals into the lakes is banned.

1972
The first Great Lakes Water Quality Agreement is established between Canada and the United States, leading to major reductions in pollution.

What Have You Learned?

True or False?

Decide whether the following statements are true or false. If the statement is false, make it true.

1. There are four Great Lakes.
2. Lake Michigan is the only Great Lake that is entirely within the United States.
3. French settlers were the first inhabitants to live near the Great Lakes.
4. Lake sturgeon populations have been affected by human activities.
5. Lake Erie is the largest of the Great Lakes.

ANSWERS

1. False. There are five Great Lakes. They are Superior, Erie, Michigan, Ontario, and Huron.
2. True. The other four Great Lakes straddle the border of Canada and the United States.
3. False. Aboriginal Peoples first inhabited the Great Lakes. They have lived in the region for at least 10,000 years.
4. True. Lake sturgeon are a threatened species due to pollution, agriculture, and other human activities.
5. False. Lake Superior is the largest of the Great Lakes.

Short Answer

Answer the following questions using information from the book.

1. What are some major threats to the wildlife in the Great Lakes?
2. How were the Great Lakes formed?
3. How many people live around the Great Lakes?
4. What passageway connects the Great Lakes to the Atlantic Ocean?
5. What is unique about the Great Lakes?

ANSWERS

1. Pollution, human activities, and invasive species
2. Erosion by glaciers
3. About 40 million people
4. The St. Lawrence Seaway
5. They are the largest group of freshwater lakes in the world.

Multiple Choice

Choose the best answer for the following questions.

1. Which of the Great Lakes is the deepest?
   a) Lake Superior
   b) Lake Michigan
   c) Lake Erie
   d) Lake Ontario

2. Which American state does not have any coast along the Great Lakes?
   a) Wisconsin
   b) New York
   c) New Jersey
   d) Illinois

3. Who was the first person to map the eastern Great Lakes?
   a) Louis Joliet
   b) Étienne Brûlé
   c) Jean Nicolet
   d) Samuel de Champlain

4. What is a major cause of pollution to the Great Lakes?
   a) pesticides
   b) fertilizers
   c) industrial waste
   d) all of the above

ANSWERS

1. a
2. c
3. d
4. d

Find Out for Yourself

Books

Spring, Barbara. *The Dynamic Great Lakes.* Independence Books, 2002.

Weatherbee, Ellen Elliot. *Guide to Great Lakes Coastal Plants.* Ann Arbor, Michigan: University of Michigan Press/Regional, 2006.

Websites

Use the Internet to find out more about the environment, people, plants, and animals of the Great Lakes.

Great Lakes Information Network
www.great-lakes.net/teach/geog/intro/intro_1.html
This site provides general information about the Great Lakes.

Great Lakes Kids
www.on.ec.gc.ca/greatlakes/For_Kids-WS4DB7BBAD-1_En.htm
Visit this site for interactive games about the Great Lakes.

Unites States Environmental Protection Agency
www.epa.gov/greatlakes/invasive/index.html
On this site, you can find information about invasive species and their effects on the Great Lakes.

Skill Matching Page

What did you learn? Look at the questions in the "Skills" column. Compare them to the page number of the answers in the "Page" column. Refresh your memory by reading the "Answer" column below.

SKILLS	ANSWER	PAGE
What facts did I learn from this book?	I learned that the Great Lakes are the largest group of freshwater lakes in the world. They are home to many animals and people.	4, 10, 12, 18
What skills did I learn?	I learned how to read a map.	5, 7, 16–17
What activities did I do?	I answered the questions in the quizzes.	7, 28–29
How can I find out more?	I can find books in the library and visit the websites in the Find Out for Yourself section.	30
How can I get involved?	I can visit websites to learn more about how to protect the Great Lakes.	30

Glossary

algae: plant-like organisms living in water that do not have stems, roots, or leaves

circumference: the distance around a place or thing at its widest point

crustaceans: animals that have hard-shelled bodies and jointed legs

economy: the resources and wealth of a place

ecosystems: communities of organisms and the environment in which they live

endangered: in danger of no longer existing any place on Earth

eroded: worn away or ground down

Great Lakes Basin: the land that contains all of the water that flows into the Great Lakes

Ice Age: a time in which most of Earth was covered with ice

immigrating: moving from one place to another

invasive species: non-native plants and animals that damage the ecosystem when they are introduced into the area

migratory: to move from one area to another

Pleistocene Epoch: time period from 2,000,000 to 10,000 years ago

quadrillion: a thousand times one trillion, or the number 1 with 15 zeros after it

sediment: sand or silt gradually deposited by wind or water and compacted to become hard

species: a specific group of plants or animals that share the same features

Index